THE MYSTERY OF...

THE LOCH NESS MONSTER

BY
HARRIETTE ABELS

EDITED BY
Dr. Howard Schroeder
*Professor in Reading and Language Arts
Dept. of Curriculum and Instruction
Mankato State University*

PUBLISHED BY
CRESTWOOD HOUSE

CIP

LIBRARY OF CONGRESS CATALOGING IN PUBLICATION DATA

Abels, Harriette Sheffer.
  The Loch Ness monster.

(The Mystery of ——)
  SUMMARY: Suggests theories relating to a large creature inhabiting Scotland's Loch Ness, reportedly sighted 3000 times since 1933.
  1. Loch Ness monster—Juvenile literature. [1. Loch Ness Monster] I. Schroeder, Howard. II. Title. III. Title: Loch Ness monster. IV. Series.
QL89.2.L6A24   1987   001.9'44   87-9027
ISBN 0-89686-343-3

International Standard Book Number:	Library of Congress Catalog Card Number:
0-89686-343-3	87-9027

CREDITS

Illustrations:
Cover Photo: Fortean Picture Library
AP/Wide World Photos: 4, 13, 18, 23, 40-41
Bob Williams: 7, 24-25, 27, 28-29, 33
British Tourist Authority: 10
Dr. Roy P. Mackal: 14, 17, 34-35, 36-37, 39
UPI/Bettmann Newsphotos: 21, 30-31
British Columbia Tourism: 43
Peter R. Hornby: 44-45
Graphic Design & Production:
Baker Street Productions, Ltd.

CRESTWOOD HOUSE

Box 3427, Mankato, MN, U.S.A. 56002

THE LOCH NESS MONSTER

TABLE OF CONTENTS

Shown above are the ruins of Urquhart Castle on the shore of Loch Ness at Inverness, Scotland.

Chapter 1

The lake is deep and dark. There are tall pine trees all around. The deserted ruins of Urquhart Castle crouch on a rocky headland along the south shore. The lake is called Loch Ness.

The wild and beautiful countryside of the Highlands in northern Scotland is dotted with many lochs (lakes). Loch Lomond is famous because of a song written about it. Loch Ness is famous because it has a monster!

For centuries the local people have told stories of the "great beastie" that lives in the lake. In olden times Loch Ness was known as *Loch Nabeiste,* "Lake of the Monster." People have been seeing the monster for more than fourteen hundred years.

The monster has been called by many names: "water horse," "water kelpie," and "beastie." Today, everyone refers to it as "Nessie."

The highlanders who live in the area of the loch are not a talkative people. For years they didn't want to talk about Nessie to outsiders. They didn't want to be laughed at. But they knew there was something strange in their loch. There were stories that dated back hundreds of years—and new sightings of the monster all the time.

In 565 A.D. a book was written called *The Latin Life of the Great Saint Columba*. That book tells the story of the day the saint met a "water monster." When Saint Columba arrived on the shore of the loch, the monster had just killed a man. But even so, Saint Columba asked one of his men to swim across the lake and bring back a boat from the opposite bank. As the man was swimming, the monster suddenly swam up to the surface, his mouth gaping wide. With a great roar it rushed toward the man swimming in the middle of the loch. Everyone standing along the shore was struck with terror. But the saint raised his hand and commanded the savage beast, "You will go no further. Do not touch the man. Turn back." Hearing this, the beast, "as if pulled back with ropes," turned away and disappeared. Since then there have been four thousand documented sightings of the creature.

In a book called *The Chronicals of Scotland* (1500 A.D.), the monster is called a dragon. One day, a man was out hunting. He used a bow and arrow to kill a strange beast "without feet, having a fin on one side, a tail, and a terrible head." The man's hunting dogs would not go near the dead animal.

If there is a monster in Loch Ness, how did it get there? Saint Columba first wrote about the monster in the sixth century, but the people living around the loch knew that Nessie was there long before. Of course, it isn't possible that today's Nessie is the same creature as the one seen in ancient times. No creature could live that long. Today's Nessie would have to be a descendant of that earlier monster.

Loch Ness is twenty-four miles (39 km) long, but only about a mile (1.6 km) wide. Until 1970, it was thought that the lake was about 754 feet (230 m) deep.

Loch Ness is twenty-four miles (39 km) long and about one mile (1.6 km) wide.

But explorations done at that time showed there are two places in the lake which are about nine hundred feet (274 m) deep. The water at that depth is very cold, but the loch itself never freezes. Visibility under the water is very poor due to a great amount of peat, silt and mud from the highland peat bogs. The plant life, which needs light to grow, is found only in the upper twenty to thirty feet (6-9 m) of the water. Millions of salmon and eels migrate annually into the loch from the North Sea.

Thousands of years ago, Loch Ness did not exist in the shape it is today. It was part of the North Sea. Then came an ice age. Land rose from underneath the water. This formed the many lakes in the area. Before this ice age, the waters of Loch Ness were salty. Now it holds fresh water.

One theory as to how the ancestors of our modern Nessie came to live in Loch Ness is explained by this change in the shape of the land and the formation of the lochs. People who believe this theory think the monster was trapped there.

Loch Ness is not the only place where monsters have been sighted; it is just the most famous one. Some people think there are underwater passageways between Loch Ness and Loch Morar or Loch Ruthven. Loch Morar has its own famous beastie called "Morag." Could Nessie and Morag be the same creature? Or are they sisters or cousins? No one knows.

Chapter 2

Until 1933, very few tourists came to Loch Ness. Now, about fifty thousand people come each year, hoping to see Nessie. Before, fishermen were about the only strangers who visited the lake. There was only one road anywhere near the lake. It had been built along the southwest shore in 1715. It wasn't close enough to the water for travelers to have a good view of the lake. Then in 1933, a new road was built along the northwest shore. This road is close to the water. Building a road is a noisy job. There is a lot of digging and blasting going on. The strange noises must have disturbed Nessie in her quiet lake. There were more than fifty sightings of the beastie that year alone!

The *Inverness Courier* was the first newspaper to call Nessie "the Loch Ness Monster." The newspaper printed the story of a couple who were driving along the new road in April of 1933. They said the lake water looked like a smooth, black mirror. Suddenly they saw a rounded hump in a patch of white foam. Then a neck with a small head on top emerged from the water. They said the animal was very big, black and shiny. They guessed that it was about sixty feet (18 m) long.

That summer, other people saw "black humps" in

This photo shows the "black humps" on what may be Nessie.

the lake. Sometimes the hump merely surfaced through the water. Other times it traveled across the lake at great speed.

In July of that year, a couple from London were driving on the south shore road. They reported seeing the monster out of the water!

"Suddenly we saw a trunk-like thing come out of the tall ferns from the hillside on our right," they said. "We were about two hundred yards (183 m) away. As it crossed the road, we could see that this trunk was really a very long neck which moved rapidly up and down. We did not see any feet. It came from the hillside. When the thing was broadside, it took up the whole road. We measured the road and found it to be twenty feet (6 m) wide."

They said it was a strange "elephant-grey" color. As they watched, the beast moved off the road and down the hillside into the loch about twenty feet (6 m) away. The couple talked to a man on a bicycle nearby about what they had just seen. A friend of his also had seen the beast and had been laughed at by the people of the village.

When the couple returned to London, they told their story to the city newspapers. Of course, the Londoners laughed at them. But all that summer and early fall there were additional sightings of the monster. Newspaper reporters traveled to Scotland hoping to see the beast, but none did.

Scientists laughed at the idea of a monster. One of them said it was a seal. Another thought it was a large otter. Then, in November, a man named Hugh Gray from a nearby village was taking a walk. He was on a bluff overlooking the lake. Suddenly he saw something move in the water. Fortunately, he had a camera with him. When the picture was developed, it was not clear, but it definitely showed something moving in the water. The something had a long body with two knobs on the side.

Everyone who saw the picture had a different idea about what it was. The guesses ranged from a bottle-nosed whale to a large, dead tree. But no matter how the scientists and news reporters laughed, people kept seeing the monster.

There have been thousands of sightings of the Loch Ness monster. In 1973, an English farmer and his wife retired to a house on Loch Ness about twelve yards (11 m) above the level of the loch. At this point in the lake, the water is only ten to twenty feet (3-6 m) deep.

One morning the farmer tried to start a tractor that had been stuck on a piece of rough ground sloping down to the edge of the loch. As the tractor started, there was a loud noise—so loud that his wife heard it in the house fifty yards (46 m) away. Right afterwards the farmer heard a loud splash, as if something heavy had been thrown in the water. It was a single noise and not followed by any more splashing sounds. The farmer thought someone had thrown a heavy object into the water. Two minutes later he saw a ring of circles, and a little to his left an animal surfaced quietly and smoothly, then submerged ''on its tail''—that is, it went straight down. The farmer said the object was rigid, like a pole, and its motion through the water was very smooth. Its color was black, and he saw a head with large scales on top and what seemed to be a slit mouth. The creature did not appear to have a neck. Above the mouth was an eye, or possibly some type of opening.

The eye was very small in proportion to the mouth. The farmer saw no sign of fins or horns.

One of the strangest stories connected with Nessie has to do with the death of a famous water racer. John Cobb was known as the fastest man on earth because he held the land speed record. He brought a jet-propelled boat to Loch Ness to try and set a water speed record. One of the reasons Cobb chose Loch Ness was the surface calm of the loch. When Cobb had the boat up to 205 miles (330 km) per hour, strange ripples suddenly appeared in front of it. The speeding boat hit the waves and bounced, exploding on contact. Cobb was killed. For many people, there was no doubt that Nessie caused the tragedy.

In 1952, John Cobb was killed at Loch Ness when unexpected waves on the lake caused his speedboat to explode.

Chapter 3

People have been trying to get a picture of Nessie for years. The most famous one was taken by Dr. Wilson. He first saw something strange about two to three hundred yards (183-274 m) from shore. As the head of an animal came out of the water, he ran to his car for his camera. He took four pictures of something moving through the water. Finally, the animal simply disappeared back into the loch. For years this picture was accepted

If Nessie has three humps, it may look like the creature in this drawing.

as the best proof that there is indeed some kind of animal living in Loch Ness.

Recently two scientists disagreed with this theory. One says the picture is of a large otter. The other says it is a diving bird.

There are other pictures that seem to show either a flipper or a fin on the monster.

In 1951, a local woodsman, who worked for the Forestry Commission, lived in a cottage some thirty yards (27 m) above the loch's surface on the southwest side. One morning, when he got up to milk his cow, he happened to look outside. He thought he saw a power boat moving in the center of the loch. Then he saw that it was moving too fast to be a boat. That's when he realized he was seeing a long, rounded hump with a second hump behind. The woodsman shouted for his wife and picked up a box camera before rushing down to the shore. By then, the object was within fifty yards (46 m) of the man.

He saw, and photographed, three humps. The head and neck, which looked like a sheep's, dropped down into the water every now and then. It turned with a splashing movement and withdrew to the center of the loch. There it sank under water. The woodsman believed that the head, neck and humps belonged to one animal. However, it could have been three separate animals moving together. Each of the animals would have been about twenty feet (6 m) long. From the photo, it seems as if the middle hump is closer to the camera than the other two. Also, the humps do not seem to be in a straight line.

The woodsman's photo is important because it is very similar to one taken by an English engineer in 1960. His name is Tim Dinsdale. Mr. Dinsdale took a movie camera to the lake, and spent several months trying to get a photograph of the monster. When he finally did, the film was studied by experts in the Royal Air Force. They decided that the hump was probably a living thing, not less than six feet (1.8 m) wide and five feet (1.5 m) high. The hump was twelve to sixteen feet (3.7-5 m) long.

From this point on, scientists took the Loch Ness monster seriously. The Loch Ness Phenomena Investigation Bureau was formed. It analyzed all the previous sightings of the beast. The analysis included newspaper reports and pictures taken since 1933. Investigators set up underwater microphones, hoping to catch a strange sound. In 1963, they exploded dynamite in the lake, hoping it would bring Nessie to the surface the way the road building did in 1933.

The chairman of the World Wildlife Fund gave Nessie a zoological name. He called her *Nessiteras rhombopteryx.*

Sonar was the next tool used to track Nessie. Sonar works by means of sonic and supersonic sound waves bouncing off an underwater object. Commercial fishing vessels use sonar to locate shoals of fish. The navy uses

These men hoped to track Nessie with a special sonar device.

it to detect enemy submarines.

The first tracking of Nessie by sonar was not pre-planned. A commercial boat was passing through the loch. It was using sonar as a depth finder. Suddenly, something strange turned up on the chart. A large form was moving between the boat and the bottom of the loch at a depth of about 480 feet (146 m). Over the next twenty years, many other boat crews also reported unusual chart records.

In the 1960's, three university expeditions installed

This sonar image shows an object on the bottom of Loch Ness that is about thirty feet (9 m) long.

sonar gear at Loch Ness, but they found nothing. It wasn't until the late '60's and early '70's, when better sonar equipment was used, that positive results finally were obtained.

The University of Birmingham, Alabama, conducted experiments that definitely prove there are many large twenty-foot (6 m) objects swimming in Loch Ness at speeds up to seventeen mph (27 kmph). They dive at rates up to five mph (8 kmph). The way they move up and down, their speed and size have led people to believe they cannot be the regular fish of the loch. The pattern of the objects' movements has caused some scientists to believe they are non-airbreathing animals with homes along the bottom and sides of the loch.

The animals sometimes swim in groups. One group of five to eight animals was tracked for almost fifteen minutes.

Because of the large amount of peat in the loch, it is difficult to see and photograph them under water. In 1969, an American scientist brought a mini-sub to Loch Ness, hoping to spot the monster. But this proved to be a poor idea, since the mini-sub was too slow and could not keep up with the monster.

In the 1970's, many scientists were still saying there was no such thing as a creature in the waters of Loch Ness. But the evidence of the photographs, the motion pictures, and the sonar scannings was simply too clear to ignore.

The American Academy of Applied Science began working in the loch in 1970. The American scientists have taken many pictures and sonar soundings, but they have been unable to present any absolute evidence.

In Rochester, New York, is a firm called Iscan. There, scientists developed a system that tracks ships electronically. They also spend a lot of time hunting the Loch Ness monster. In 1983, the two men who run the company flew to Scotland hoping to find Nessie. They set up 144 sonar devices covering an area of 6,400 sq. feet (5,952 sq. m). They also installed nine underwater dart guns. Any object more than ten feet (3 m) long that came near the devices would set off an alarm. The sonar would track the object and the dart guns would fire at it. That way, scientists could examine any animal tissue in the tips of the dart guns. But after six weeks of continuous tracking, there wasn't even a peep on the alarm system.

Chapter 4

Nessie has been described in many ways. Some say it has flippers like a seal. Others say it has a long neck and small horns. Still other reports describe humps like a camel. Sometimes it appears in a huge wake of white foam. Other times Nessie streaks through the water like a motorboat. Sometimes the monster's head suddenly appears through the stillness of the lake's surface. Other times it raises up with a huge shower of water spraying in all directions.

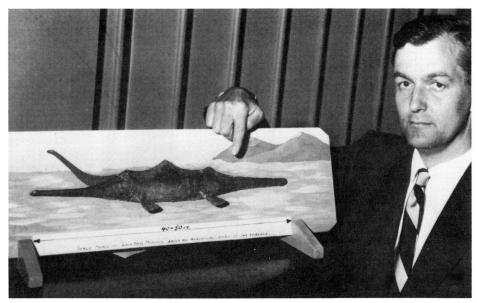

Tim Dinsdale claims he saw Nessie in 1960. He is shown here with a model he made of the creature.

The food supply in Loch Ness is plentiful. The descriptions of the quiet hump suddenly moving off at great speed could be explained as a form of fishing. The monster waits until the fish get near, then when it spots its prey, it dashes off to eat it up.

One of the most confusing things about the description of Nessie is the disagreement in reports of its shape. Some say there is a single, rounded hump, sometimes smooth or sometimes with a ridge. Other times, two humps are seen. Sometimes, three parts are seen. This third part has been identified either as a head-neck or as a third hump. The hump has been seen moving back and forth rapidly. This evidence of humps, or up-and-down ripples, has been confirmed by sonar traces. The small limbs that have been described must be used for steering and swimming. They are definitely not much good for walking.

In 1972, Dr. Robert H. Rines took several pictures of Nessie with an underwater camera. The pictures clearly show what look like flippers, similar to those on seals and other aquatic mammals.

Descriptions of horns or antennae are rare, and no one has ever reported seeing any ears. Some people have said that the animal continually opened and closed its mouth and that its throat seemed to vibrate and pulse. It has been described as tossing its head from side to side. Sometimes observers say the creature is black and slimy; other times it appears dark brown or grey. Its

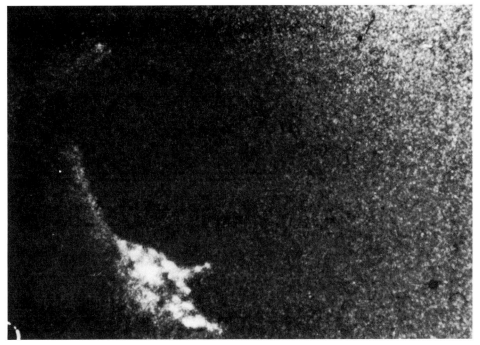

This underwater photograph, taken in 1976, shows what appear to be flippers on some kind of animal.

size seems to range from that of a large cow to a creature about thirty feet (9 m) in length.

We know from the sonar charts that whatever the creature is, it can dive much like a seal does. It can also move along the surface and under water at speeds of ten miles per hour (16 kmph) or more. This has been established by film and sonar. To swim this fast, it must have a powerful tail. This would also go along with the awkward movements the animal seems to have when moving over land.

The most popular theory is that the Loch Ness monster is a modern form of plesiosaur, a marine reptile thought to be extinct. Maybe Nessie looks like this artist's impression.

24

Chapter 5

Nessie has also been seen on land from time to time.

In 1933, a woman saw a dark gray mass on the beach, twenty to twenty-five feet (6-7.6 m) in length. Its back looked ridged and had several humps on it. It had short, thick, clumsy legs with hoofs like a pig's, only larger. She said it did not stand on its legs, but kept its hind legs on the ground like a seal.

That year, another woman described a strange animal resting on the slope of the loch shore. It seemed to have a hairy mane on its neck. The rest of the body seemed hairy, too. The woman thought it was shaped like a hippopotamus, with a large, round head and short, thick legs.

The following year, a man saw a creature with a small head and a long neck. Its bulky body had two slight humps and a long tail that was rounded at the end. Its head looked like an eel's head with large eyes. The creature had four flippers, the front flippers seeming to be very strong. The man reported that it loped across the road like a sea lion, arching its back.

Also in 1934, two women saw an animal crossing a stream by moonlight, moving toward the loch and out of sight. It had a thick upper body that tapered toward

In 1934, two women saw an animal crossing a stream by moonlight. This is an artist's image of what they saw.

a tail. It was dark in color, but the underside of its neck was white. It had four short legs and moved very quickly.

In 1960, a man saw a gray-black mass near the loch. Using binoculars, he saw an animal that he guessed to be about forty-five feet (13.7 m) in length. It had one pair of paddles. But as the animal turned to flop back into the water, the man thought he saw a third square-ended flipper that looked almost like an elephant's trunk.

The man wasn't sure whether he had seen the head and neck or the tail end of the creature. And when he drew sketches of the creature for scientists, they thought that the ''limbs'' could have been either front or rear.

In 1960, a man claimed to have seen Nessie. This drawing is based on his description of the lake monster.

Interestingly, the man's sketches show the third square-ended flipper in the same location claimed by others who have supposedly seen the monster.

There is one explanation for the sightings that has nothing to do with any animal. Scientists have suggested that tremors of the earth or slight earthquakes may release gas bubbles from the floor of the lake. This would account for what look like humps.

Another scientist has suggested that mats of vegetation might account for the sightings. But plant material is very sparse in Loch Ness. It would be difficult for a mat of such large size to form.

This 1934 photo shows waves that were supposedly made by Nessie. Today, experts say that small earthquakes could release gas from the floor of the lake, causing the same kind of waves.

Chapter 6

If there is a Nessie, what can it be? There are otters in Loch Ness, and perhaps some of the sightings were of otters. But no known otter can dive to seven hundred feet (213 m).

The elephant seal is big enough to be the monster. Also, an elephant seal could live in the temperature of the loch. But these animals give birth on land, not in the water. If Nessie were a type of seal, it would be seen on land more often.

Modern whales, dolphins and porpoises do not come up on land. Neither are their necks elongated. Nessie cannot be that kind of creature.

It was once thought that Nessie might be a type of reptile. But Nessie spends most of its time at the bottom or around the sides of the loch, where the temperature is only ten degrees F above freezing (-12 C). Reptiles do not like freezing temperature.

Scientists have suggested that perhaps the beastie has developed a special adaptation to this low temperature. That has happened before. In fact, the leatherback or green turtle does show just such a temperature adaptation.

There are some scientists who believe Nessie may be an invertebrate. An invertebrate is an animal without

Some scientists believe Nessie could be an invertebrate, which is an animal without a backbone.

a backbone. This would account for the monster's large size and the strange humping movements so often reported by witnesses.

In 1933, an American naturalist thought that Nessie might be a giant squid. It has since been suggested that it may be a large worm-like creature.

Nessie might also be a giant amphibian. Frogs and

Experts have tried almost everything to find out what Nessie looks like. In this photo, the Viperfish, a small submarine, prepares to dive. No definite sightings were ever made from the sub.

newts are amphibians. Most modern amphibians are very small. But thousands of years ago, there were huge amphibians, about fifteen feet (4.6 m) long, that had four small feet. Fossils of these animals have been found in Scotland. This type of amphibian supposedly has been extinct for thousands of years.

Roy P. Mackal teaches at the University of Chicago.

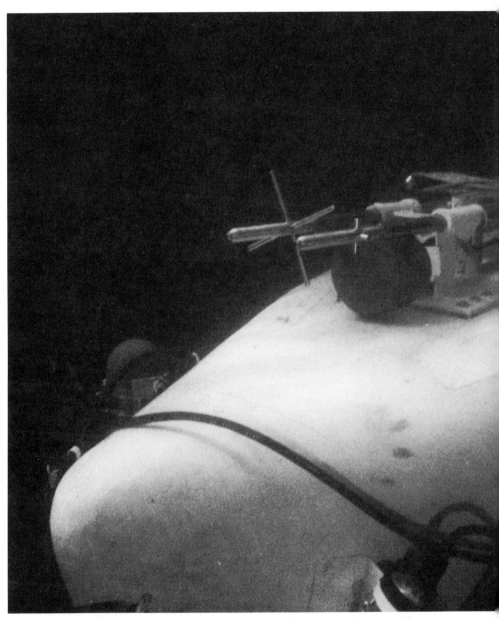

The Viperfish was even equipped with special harpoons that could have collected skin tissue from Nessie.

He is very involved in searching for the Loch Ness monster. Dr. Mackal believes that Nessie is a primitive snake-like whale belonging to the supposedly extinct group, *archeoceti*.

The most popular scientific theory is that the loch monster is a modern form of *plesiosaur*. A plesiosaur had a long neck, flippers, and a hump. It lived on a fish diet, and was about twenty feet (6 m) in length. Some types of plesiosaurs were also believed to swim at rapid speeds, and give birth to their young in the water. There is only one problem with this theory. The plesiosaur has been extinct for several thousand years! At least, we think so.

There have been other cases where scientists thought a species was extinct and then discovered that it wasn't. The *coelacanth* is a primitive fish that was believed to be extinct. Then, some were discovered off the coast of Africa.

A *neopilina* is a small, primitive mollusk that was also supposed to be extinct. However, it was found living in 1957. That leads some scientists to believe Nessie may be an evolved form of a plesiosaur, living in Loch Ness.

What do we know for sure about Nessie? The number of recorded sightings since 1933 is about three thousand. A large percentage of these probably are errors, mistakes, or even practical jokes. Ducks, birds, otters, and even small fishing boats and floating logs have been mistaken for the monster. But allowing for all of these

When this boat approached an object making a wave in 1968, the object disappeared. Events like this keep scientists interested!

errors, there appears to be enough evidence to be quite sure that something . . . or many things . . . do, indeed, live in the cold waters of Loch Ness.

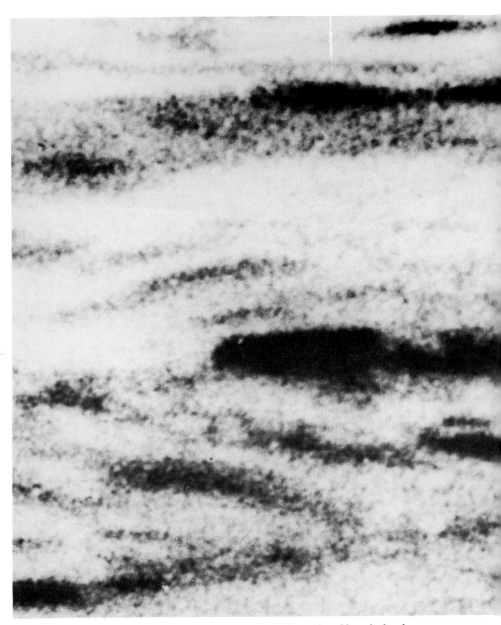

This photo was taken on Loch Ness in 1961. Is this what Nessie looks like?

40

Chapter 7

Scotland is not the only country that has "water monsters." In Ireland the beasts are called "plasts." In Wales there is an ancient legend about a monster called "Afanc." In the northern part of Sweden people talk about a Great Lake Monster that sounds almost like Nessie. And folktales in Sweden and Norway tell of giant "worms" that used to frighten sailors.

Russia has several lakes where long-necked beasts have been seen. A team of Russian geologists saw one such beast at Lake Khaiyr in Siberia in 1964. They first saw the beast on land and then saw it swimming in the lake. Their description of the monster sounds like Nessie: black, with a long neck and a small head. It had a long body with a long tail and dorsal fin. Other Russian lake monsters have been described as looking like dinosaurs.

Lake monsters also have been seen in North America. Many people have reported seeing strange beasts in Lake Champlain in upper New York State. Strange creatures have also been seen in several Canadian lakes as well. The most famous Canadian monster is Ogopogo. This has been sighted in Lake Okanagan in British Columbia. There is even a statue of Ogopogo on the shore of the lake.

A statue of Ogopogo has been erected on the shore of Lake Okanagan in British Columbia.

After all the "sightings," searches, and scientific theories, there still is no definite answer to the big question: Are there such creatures as lake monsters?

We don't yet know. But a great many people are spending time and money trying to find out.

Is there a "monster" somewhere in Loch Ness? A definite answer is yet to be found.

Map

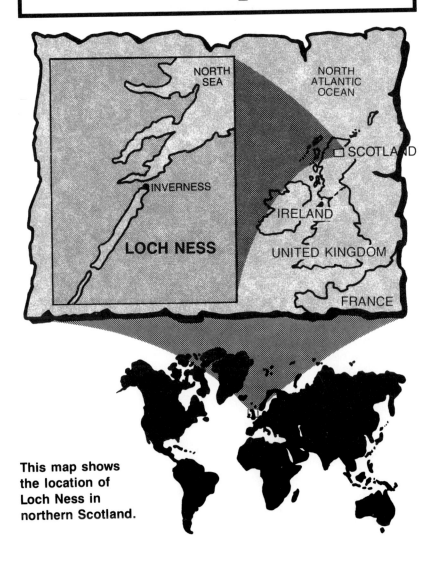

NORTH SEA

NORTH ATLANTIC OCEAN

□ SCOTLAND

INVERNESS

IRELAND

LOCH NESS

UNITED KINGDOM

FRANCE

This map shows
the location of
Loch Ness in
northern Scotland.

Glossary/Index

47